RUDOLF JOSEPH LORENZ STEINER was an Austrian occultist, social reformer, architect, esotericist, and claimed clairvoyant. Steiner gained initial recognition at the end of the nineteenth century as a literary critic and published works including The Philosophy of Freedom.

RUDOLF STEINER

A ROAD TO SELF-KNOWLEDGE

DELHI OPEN BOOKS

Contents

INTRODUCTORY REMARKS

IT is the endeavour of this treatise to convey spiritual-scientific knowledge concerning the being of man. The method of representation is arranged in such a way that the reader may grow into what is depicted, so that, in the course of reading, it becomes for him a kind of self-conference. If this soliloquy takes on such a form that thereby hitherto concealed forces, which can be awakened in every soul, reveal themselves, then the reading leads to a real inner work of the soul; and the latter can see itself gradually urged on to that soul-journeying, which truly advances towards the beholding of the spiritual world.

What has to be imparted, therefore, has been given in the form of eight Meditations, which can be actually practised. If this is done, they can be adapted for imparting to the soul, through its own inner deepening, that about which they speak.

It has been my aim on the one hand, to give something to those readers who have already made themselves conversant with the literature dealing with the domain of the supersensible, as it is here understood.

Thus through the style of the description, through the communication directly connecting with the soul's experience, perhaps those who have knowledge of supersensible life will here find something that may appear of importance to them.

On the other hand, many a one can find that just through this method of representation profit may be gained by those who yet stand far distant from the achievements of Spiritual Science.

Although this work is intended as an amplification of my other writings in the domain of Spiritual Science, it should nevertheless be possible to read it independently.

It has been my endeavour in my books, Theosophy and Occult Science, to represent the things as they show themselves to observation, when it ascends to the Spiritual. In these works the method of representation is descriptive and its direction prescribed by conformity to the law manifesting out of the things themselves.

In this, A Road to Self-Knowledge, the method of representation is different. Herein is stated that which can be experienced by a soul which sets out on the path to the Spirit in a certain manner.

The treatise may therefore be regarded as an account of experiences of the soul; only it must be taken into consideration that the experiences which can be gained in such a way as is here described, must assume an individual form in each soul according to its own peculiarity. It has been my endeavour to do justice to this fact, so that one can also imagine that what is depicted here has been actually lived through by an individual soul, exactly as represented.

The title of this treatise is, therefore, A Road to Self-knowledge.

On that account it may serve the purpose of assisting other souls to live into this portrayal and attain to corresponding goals, and is an amplification of my book, Knowledge of the Higher Worlds and its Attainment.

Only isolated fundamental experiences of a spiritual scientific nature are represented. The giving of information in this manner of the further spheres of "Spiritual Science" is suspended for the present.

RUDOLF STEINER.

Munich

August 1912

FIRST MEDITATION

In which the Attempt is made to obtain a True Idea of the Physical Body WHEN the soul is surrendered to the phenomena of the outer world by means of physical perception, it cannot be said - after true self-analysis - that the soul perceives these phenomena, or that it actually experiences the things of the outer world. For, during the time of surrender, in its devotion to the outer world, the soul knows in truth nothing of itself. The fact is rather that the sunlight itself, radiating from things through space in various colours, lives or experiences itself within the soul. When the soul enjoys any event, at the moment of enjoyment it actually is joy in so far as it is conscious of being anything. Joy experiences itself in the soul. The soul is one with its experience of the world. It does not experience itself as something separate which feels joy, admiration, delight, satisfaction, or fear. It actually is joy, admiration, delight, satisfaction, and fear. If the soul would always admit this fact, then and only then would the occasions when it retires from the experience of the outer world and contemplates itself by itself appear in the right light. These moments would then appear as forming a life of quite a special character, which at once shows itself to be entirely different from the ordinary life of the soul. It is with this special kind of life that the riddles of the soul's existence begin to dawn upon our consciousness. And these riddles are, in fact, the source of all other riddles of the world. For two worlds - an outer and an inner - present themselves to the spirit of man, directly the soul for a longer or shorter time ceases to be one with the outer world and withdraws into the loneliness of its own existence.

Now this withdrawal is no simple process, which, having been once accomplished, may be repeated again in much the same way. It is much more like the beginning of a pilgrimage into worlds previously unknown. When once this pilgrimage has been begun, every step made will call forth others, and will also be the preparation for these others. It is the first step which makes the soul capable of taking the next one. And each step brings fuller knowledge of the answer to the question: "What is Man in the true sense of the word?" Worlds open up which are hidden from the ordinary conception of life. And yet only in those worlds can the facts be found which will reveal the truth about this very conception. And even if no answer proves all-embracing and final the answers obtained through the soul's inner pilgrimage go beyond everything which the outer senses and the intellect bound up with them can ever give. For this " something more " is necessary to man, and he will find that this is so, when he really and earnestly analyses his own nature.

At the outset of such a pilgrimage through the realms of our own soul, hard logic and common sense are necessary. They form a safe starting-point for pushing on into the supersensible realms, which the soul, after all, is yearning to reach. Many a soul would prefer not to trouble about such a starting-point, but rather penetrate directly into the supersensible realms; though every healthy soul, even if it has at first avoided such commonsense considerations as disagreeable, will always submit to them later. For however much knowledge of the supersensible worlds one may have obtained from another starting-point, one can only gain a firm footing there through some such methods of reasoning as follow here.

In the life of the soul moments may come in which it says to itself: "You must be able to withdraw from everything that an outer world can give you, if you do not wish to be forced into confessing that you are but self- contradictory non-sense;

but this would make life impossible, because it is clear that what you perceive around you exists independently of you; it existed without you and will continue to exist without you. Why then do colours perceive themselves in you, whilst your perception may be of no consequence to them? Why do the forces and materials of the outer world build up your body? Careful thought will show that this body only acquires life as the outward manifestation of you. It is a part of the outer world transformed into you, and, moreover, you realise that it is necessary to you. Because, to begin with, you could have no inner experiences without your senses, which the body alone can put at your disposal. You would remain empty without your body, such as you are at the beginning. It gives you through the senses inner fulness and substance." And then all those reflections may follow which are essential to any human existence if it does not wish to get into unbearable contradiction with itself at certain moments which come to every human being. This body - as it exists at the present moment - is the expression of the soul's experience. Its processes are such as to allow the soul to live through it and to gain experience of itself in it.

A time will come, however, when this will not be so. The life in the body will some day be subject to laws quite different from those which it obeys to-day whilst living for you, and for the sake of your soul's experience. It will become subject to those laws, according to which the material and forces in nature are acting, laws which have nothing more to do with you and your life. The body to which you owe the experience of your soul, will be absorbed in the general world-process and exist there in a form which has nothing more in common with anything that you experience within yourself

Such a reflection may call forth in the inner experience all the horror of the thought of death, but without the admixture of the merely personal feelings which are ordinarily connected with this thought. When such personal feelings prevail it is not easy to establish the calm, deliberate state of mind necessary for obtaining knowledge. It is natural that man should want to know about death and about a life of the soul independent of the dissolution of the body. But the relation existing between man himself and these questions is - perhaps more than anything else in the world - apt to confuse his objective judgment and to make him accept as genuine answers only those which are inspired by his own desires or wishes. For it is impossible to obtain true knowledge of anything in the spiritual realms without being able with complete unconcern to accept a "No " quite as willingly as a "Yes." And we need only look conscientiously into ourselves to become distinctly aware of the fact that we do not accept the knowledge of an extinction of the life of the soul together with the death of the body with the same equanimity as the opposite knowledge which teaches the continued existence of the soul beyond death. No doubt there are people who quite honestly believe in the annihilation of the soul on the extinction of the life of the body, and who arrange their lives accordingly. But even these are not unbiased with regard to such a belief. It is true that they do not allow the fear of annihilation, and the wish for continued existence, to get the better of the reasons which are distinctly in favour of such annihilation. So far the conception of these people is more logical than that of others who unconsciously construct or accept arguments in favour of a continued existence, because there is an ardent desire in the secret depths of their souls for such continued existence. And yet the view of those who deny immortality is no less biased, only in a different way. There are amongst them some who build up a certain idea of what life and existence are. This idea forces them to think of certain conditions, without which life is impossible. Their view of existence leads them to the conclusion that the conditions of the soul's life can no longer be present when the body falls away. Such people do not notice that they have themselves from the very first fixed an idea of the conditions necessary for the existence of life, and cannot believe in a continuation of life after death for the simple reason that, according to their own preconceived idea, there is no possibility of imagining an existence without a body. Even if they are not biased by their own wishes, they are biased by their own ideas from which they cannot emancipate themselves. Much confusion still prevails in such matters, and only a few examples need be put forward of what exists in this direction. For instance, the thought that the body, through whose processes the soul manifests its life, will eventually be given over to the outer world, and follow laws which have no relation to inner life - this thought puts the experience of death before the soul in such a way that no wish, no personal consideration, need necessarily enter the mind; and by a thought such as this we are led to a simple, impersonal question of knowledge. Then also the thought will soon dawn upon the mind that the idea of death is not important in itself, but rather because it may throw light upon life. And we shall have to come to the conclusion that it is possible to understand the riddle of life through the nature of death.

The fact that the soul desires its own continued existence should, under all circumstances, make us suspicious with regard to any opinion which the soul forms about its own immortality. For why should the facts of the world pay any heed to the feelings of the soul? It is a possible thought that the soul, like a flame produced from fuel, merely flashes forth from the substance of the body and is then again extinguished. Indeed, the necessity of forming some opinion about its own nature might perhaps lead the soul to this very thought, with the result that it would feel itself to be devoid of meaning. But nevertheless this thought might be the actual truth of the matter, even although it made the soul feel itself to be meaningless.

When the soul turns its eyes to the body, it ought only to

take into consideration that which the body may reveal to it. It then seems as if in nature such laws were active as drive matter and forces into a continual process of change, and as if these laws controlled the body and after a while drew it into that general process of mutual change.

You may put this idea in any way you like: it may be scientifically admissible, but with regard to true reality it proves itself to be quite impossible. You may find it to be the only idea which seems scientifically clear and sensible, and that all the rest are only subjective beliefs. You may imagine that it is so, but you cannot adhere to this idea with a really unbiased mind. And that is the point. Not that which the soul according to its own nature feels to be a necessity, but only that which the outer world, to which the body belongs, makes evident, ought to be taken into consideration. After death this outer world absorbs the matter and forces of the body, which then follow laws that are quite indifferent to that which takes place in the body during life.

These laws (which are of a physical and chemical nature) have just the same relation to the body as they have to any other lifeless thing of the outer world. It is impossible to imagine that this indifference of the outer world with regard to the human body should only begin at the moment of death, and should not have existed during life.

An idea of the relation between our body and the physical world cannot be obtained from life, but only from impressing upon our mind the thought that everything belonging to us as a vehicle of our senses, and as the means by which the soul carries on its life - all this is treated by the physical world in a way which only becomes clear to us when we look beyond the limits of our bodily life and take into consideration that a time will come when we no longer have about us the body in which we are now gaining experience of ourselves. Any other conception of the relation between the outer physical world and the body conveys in itself the feeling of not conforming with reality. The idea, however, that it is only after death that the real relationship between the body and the outer world reveals itself does not contradict any real experience of the outer or the inner world.

The soul does not feel the thought to be unendurable, that the matter and the forces of its body are given up to processes of the outer world which have nothing to do with its own life. Surrendering itself to life in a perfectly unprejudiced way, it cannot discover in its own depths any wish arising from the body which makes the thought of dissolution after death a disagreeable one. The idea becomes unbearable only when it implies that the matter and the forces returning to the outer world take with them the soul and its experiences of its own existence. Such an idea would be unbearable for the same reason as would any other idea, which does not grow naturally out of a reliance on the manifestation of the outer world.

To ascribe to the outer world an entirely different relation to the existence of the body during life from that which it bears after death is an absolutely futile idea. As such it will always be repelled by reality, whereas the idea that the relation between the outer world and the body remains the same before and after death is quite sound. The soul, holding this latter view, feels itself in perfect harmony with the evidence of facts. It is able to feel that this idea does not clash with facts which speak for themselves, and to which no artificial thought need be added.

One does not always observe in what beautiful harmony are the natural healthy feelings of the soul with the manifestations of nature. This may seem so self-evident as not to need any remark, and yet this seemingly insignificant fact is most illuminating. The idea that the body is dissolved into the elements has nothing unbearable in it, but on the other hand, the thought that the soul shares the fate of the body is senseless. There are many human personal reasons which prove this, but such reasons must be left out of consideration in objective investigation.

Apart from these reasons, however, thoroughly impersonal attention to the teachings of the outer world shows that no different influence upon the soul can be ascribed to this outer world before death from that which it has after death. The fact is conclusive that this idea presents itself as a necessity and holds its own against all objections which may be raised against it. Any one who thinks this thought when fully self-conscious feels its direct truth. In fact, both those who deny and those who believe in immortality think in this way. The former will probably say that the conditions of the bodily processes during life are involved in the laws which act upon the body after death; but they are mistaken if they believe that they are really capable of imagining these laws to be in a different relation to the body during life when it is the vehicle of the soul from that which prevails after death.

The only idea possible in itself is that the special combination of forces which comes into existence with the body, remains quite as indifferent to the body in its character of a vehicle for the soul, as that combination of forces which produces the processes in the dead body. This indifference is not existent on the part of the soul, but on the part of the matter and the forces of the body. The soul gains experience of itself by means of the body, but the body lives with, in, and through the outer world and does not allow any more importance to the soul as such than to the processes of the outer world. One comes to the conclusion that the heat and cold of the outer world have an influence upon the circulation of the blood in our body which is analogous to that of fear and shame which exist within the soul.

So, first of all, we feel within ourselves the laws of the outer world active in that special combination of materials which manifests itself as the form of the human body. We feel this body as a member of the outer world, but remain ignorant of its inner workings. External science of the present day gives some information as to how the laws of the outer world combine within that particular entity, which presents itself as the human body. We may hope that this information will grow more complete in the future. But such increasing information can make no difference whatever to the way in which the soul has to think of its relation to the body. It will, on the contrary, bring more and more into evidence that the laws of the outer world remain in the same relation to the soul before and after death. It is an illusion to expect that the progress of the knowledge of nature will show how far the bodily processes are agents of the life of the soul. We shall more and more clearly recognise that which takes place in the body during life, but the processes in question will always be felt by the soul as being outside it in the same way as the processes in the body after death.

The body must therefore appear within the outer world as a combination of forces and substances, which exists by itself and is explainable by itself as a member of this outer world. Nature causes a plant to grow and again decomposes it. Nature rules the human body, and causes it to pass away within her own sphere. If man takes up his position to nature with such ideas, he is able to forget himself and all that is in him and feel his body as a member of the outer world. If he thinks in such a way of its relations to himself and to nature, he experiences in connection with himself that which we may call his physical body.

SECOND MEDITATION

In which the Attempt is made to form a True Conception of the Elemental or Etheric Body

THROUGH the idea which the soul has to form in connection with the fact of death, it may be driven into complete uncertainty with regard to its own being. This will be the case when it believes that it cannot obtain knowledge of any other world but the world of the senses and of that which the intellect is able to ascertain about this world. The ordinary life of the soul directs its attention to the physical body. It sees that body being absorbed after death into the workshop of nature, which has no connection with that which the soul experiences before death as its own existence. The soul may indeed know (through the preceding Meditation) that the physical body during life bears the same relation to it as after death, but this does not lead it further than to the acknowledgment of the inner independence of its own experiences up to the moment of death. What happens to the physical body after death is evident from observation of the outer world. But such observation is not possible with regard to its inner experience. In so far then as it perceives itself through the senses, the soul in its ordinary life cannot see beyond the boundary of death. If the soul is incapable of forming any ideas which go beyond that outer world which absorbs the body after death, then with regard to all that concerns its own being it is unable to look into anything but empty nothingness on the other side of death.

If this is to be otherwise, the soul must perceive the outer world by other means than those of the senses and of the intellect connected with them. These themselves belong to the body and decay together with it. What they tell us can lead to nothing but to the result of the first Meditation, and this result consists merely in the soul being able to say to itself: "I am bound to my body. This body is subject to natural laws which are related to me in the same way as all other natural laws. Through them I am a member of the outer world and a part of this world is expressed in my body, a fact which I realise most distinctly, when I consider what the outer world does to that body after death. During life it gives me senses and an intellect which make it impossible for me to see how matters stand with regard to my soul's experiences on the other side of death." Such a statement can only lead to two results. Either any further investigation into the riddle of the soul is suppressed and all efforts to obtain knowledge on this subject are given up; or else efforts are made to obtain by the inner experience of the soul that which the outer world refuses. These efforts may bring about an increase of power and energy with regard to this inner experience such as it would not have in ordinary life.

In ordinary life man has a certain amount of strength in his inner experiences, in his life of feeling and thought. He thinks, for instance, a certain thought as often as there is an inner or outer impulse to do so.

Any thought may, however, be chosen out of the rest and voluntarily repeated again and again without any outer reason, and with such intense energy as actually to make it live as an inner reality. Such a thought may by repeated effort be made the exclusive object of our inner experience. And while we do this we can keep away all outer impressions and memories which may arise in the soul. It is then possible to turn such a complete surrender to certain thoughts or feelings exclusive of all others, into a regular inner activity. If, however, such an inner experience is to lead to really important results, it must be undertaken according to certain tested laws. Such laws are recorded by the science of spiritual life. In my book Knowledge of the Higher Worlds and its Attainment, a great number of these rules or laws are mentioned. Through such methods we obtain a strengthening of the powers of inner experience. This experience becomes in a certain way condensed. What is brought about by this we learn through that observation of ourselves which sets in when the inner activity described has been continued for a sufficiently long time. It is true that much patience is required before convincing results appear. And if we are not disposed to exercise such patience for years, we shall obtain nothing of importance.

Here it is only possible to give one example of such results, for they are of many varieties. And that which is mentioned here is adapted to further the particular method of meditation which we are now describing.

A man may carry out the inner strengthening of the life of his soul which has been indicated for a long period without perhaps anything happening in his inner life which is able to alter his usual way of thinking with regard to the world. Suddenly, however, the following may occur. Naturally the incident to be described might not occur in exactly the same way to two different persons. But if we arrive at a conception of one experience of this kind, we shall have gained an understanding of the whole matter in question. A moment may occur in which the soul gets an inner experience of itself in quite a new way. At the beginning it will generally happen that the soul during sleep wakes up, as it were, in a dream. But we feel at once that this experience cannot be compared with ordinary dreams. We are completely shut off from the world of sense and intellect, and yet we feel the experience in the same way as when we are standing fully awake before the outer world in ordinary life. We feel compelled to picture the experience in ourselves. For this purpose we use ideas such as we have in ordinary life, but we know very well that we are experiencing things different from those to which such ideas are normally attached. These ideas are only used as a means of expression for an experience which we have not had before, and which we are also able to know that it is impossible for us to have in ordinary life.

We feel, for instance, as though thunderstorms were all around us. We hear thunder and see lightning. And yet we know we are in our own room. We feel permeated by a force previously quite unknown to us. Then we imagine we see rents in the walls around us, and we feel compelled to say to ourselves or to some one we think is near us. "I am now in great difficulties, the lightning is going through the house and taking hold of me; I feel it seizing and dissolving me." When such a series of representations has been gone through, the inner experience passes back to ordinary soul-conditions. We find ourselves again in ourselves with the memory of the experience just undergone. If this memory is as vivid and accurate as any other, it enables us to form an opinion of the experience. We then have a direct knowledge that we have gone through something which cannot be experienced by any physical sense nor by ordinary intelligence, for we feel that the description just given and communicated to others or to ourselves is only a means of expressing the experience. Although the expression is a means of understanding the fact of the experience, it has nothing in common with it. We know that we do not need any of our senses in having such an experience.

One who attributes it to a hidden activity of the senses or of the brain, does not know the true character of the experience. He adheres to the description which speaks of lightning, thunder, and rents in the walls, and therefore he believes that this experience of the soul is only an echo of ordinary life. He must consider the thing as a vision in the ordinary sense of the word. He cannot think otherwise. He does not take into consideration, however, that when one describes such an experience one only uses the words lightning, thunder, rents in the walls as pictures of that which has been experienced, and that one must not mistake the pictures for the experience itself. It is true that the matter appears to one as if one really saw these pictures. But one did not stand in the same relation to the phenomenon of the lightning in this case as when seeing a flash with the physical eye. The vision of the lightning is only something which, as it were, conceals the experience itself; one looks through the lightning to something beyond which is quite different, to something which cannot be experienced in the outer world of sense.

In order that a correct judgment may be made possible, it is necessary that the soul which has such experiences should, when they are over, be on a thoroughly sound footing with regard to the ordinary outer world. It must be able clearly to contrast what it has undergone as a special experience, with its ordinary experience of the outer world. Those who in ordinary life are already disposed to be carried away by all kinds of wild imaginings regarding things, are most unfit to form such a judgment. The more sound - or one might say sober - a sense of reality we have got the more likely we are to form a true and, therefore, valuable judgment of such things. One can only attain to confidence in supersensible experiences when one feels with regard to the ordinary world that one clearly perceives its processes and objects as they really are.

When all necessary conditions are thus fulfilled, and when we have reason to believe that we have not been misled by an ordinary vision, then we know that we have had an experience in which the body was not transmitting perceptions. We have had direct perception through the strengthened soul without the body. We have gained the certainty of an experience when outside the body.

It is evident that in this sphere the natural differences

A Road To Self-Knowledge

between fancy or illusion and true observation made when outside the body, cannot be indicated in any other way than in the realm of outer sense perception. It may happen that some one has a very active imagination with regard to taste, and therefore, at the mere thought of lemonade, gets the same sensation as if he were really drinking it. The difference, however, in such a case becomes evident through the association of actual circumstances in life. And so it is also with those experiences which are made when we are out of the body. In order to arrive at a fully convincing conception in this sphere, it is necessary that we should become familiar with it in a perfectly healthy way and acquire the faculty of observing the details of the experience and correcting one thing by another.

Through such an experience as the one described, we gain the possibility of observing that which belongs to our proper self not only by means of the senses and intellect - in other words, the bodily instruments. Now we not only know something more of the world than those instruments will allow of, but we know it in a different way. This is especially important. A soul that passes through an inner transformation will more and more clearly comprehend that the oppressive problems of existence cannot be solved in the world of sense because the senses and the intellect cannot penetrate deeply enough into the world as a whole. Those souls penetrate deeper which so transform themselves as to be able to have experiences when outside the body; and it is in the records which they are able to give of their experiences that the means for solving the riddles of the soul can be found.

Now an experience that occurs when outside the body is of a quite different nature from one made when in the body. This is shown by the very opinion which may be formed about the experiences described, when, after it is over, the ordinary waking condition of the soul is re-established and memory has come into a vivid and clear condition. The physical body is felt by the soul as separated from the rest of the world, and seems only to have a real existence in so far as it belongs to the soul. It is not so, however, with that which we experience within ourselves and with regard to ourselves when outside the body, for then we feel ourselves linked to all that may be called the outer world. All our surroundings are felt as belonging to us just as our hands do in the world of sense. There is no indifference to the world outside us when we come to the inner soul-world. We feel ourselves completely grown together, and woven into one with that which here may be called the world. Its activities are actually felt streaming through our own being. There is no sharp boundary line between an inner and an outer world. The whole environment belongs to the observing soul just as our two physical hands belong to our physical head.

In spite of this, however, we may say that a certain part of this outer world belongs more to ourselves than the rest of the environment, in the same way in which we speak of the head as independent of the hands or feet. Just as the soul calls a piece of the outer physical world its body, so when living outside the body it may also consider a part of the supersensible outer world as belonging to it. When we penetrate to an observation of the realm accessible to us beyond the world of the senses, we may very well say that a body unperceived by the senses belongs to us. We may call this body the elemental or etheric body, but in using the word "etheric" we must not allow any connection with that fine matter which science calls "ether" to establish itself in our mind.

Just as the mere reflection upon the connection between man and the outer world of nature leads to a conception of the physical body which agrees with facts, so does the pilgrimage of the soul into realms that can be perceived outside the physical body lead to the recognition of an elemental or etheric body, or body of formative forces.

THIRD MEDITATION

In which the Attempt is made to form an Idea of Clairvoyant Cognition of the Elemental World

WHEN we have perceptions by means of the elemental body and not through the physical senses, we experience a world that remains unknown to perception of the senses and to ordinary intellectual thinking. If we wish to compare this world with something belonging to ordinary life, we shall find nothing more appropriate than the world of memory. Just as recollections emerge from the innermost soul, so also do the supersensible experiences of the elemental body. In the case of a memory-picture the soul knows that it is related to an earlier experience in the world of the senses. In a similar way the supersensible conception implies a relation. Just as the recollection by its very nature presents itself as something which cannot be described as a mere picture of the imagination, so does also the supersensible conception. The latter wrests itself from the soul's experience, but manifests itself immediately as an inner experience that is related to something external. It is by means of recollection that a past experience becomes present to the soul. But it is by means of a supersensible conception that something, which at some time can be found somewhere in the supersensible world, becomes an inner experience of the soul. The very nature of Supersensible conceptions impresses upon our mind that they are to be looked upon as communications from a supersensible world manifesting within the soul.

How far we get in this way with our experiences in the supersensible world depends upon the amount of energy we apply to the strengthening of the life of our soul.

The attainment of the conviction that a plant is not merely that which we perceive in the world of the senses as well as the attainment of such a conviction with regard to the whole earth belongs to the same sphere of supersensible experience. If any one who has acquired the faculty of perception when outside his physical body, looks at a plant, he will be able to perceive - besides what his senses are showing him - a delicate form which permeates the whole plant. This form presents itself as an entity of force; and he is brought to consider this entity as that which builds up the plant from the materials and forces of the physical world, and which brings about the circulation of the sap. He may say - employing an available, although not an altogether appropriate simile - that there is something in the plant which sets the sap in motion in the same way as that in which his own soul moves his arm. He looks upon something internal in the plant, and he must allow a certain independence to this inner principle of the plant in its relation to that part which is perceived by the senses. He must also admit that this inner principle existed before the physical plant existed. Then if he continues to observe how a plant grows, withers, and produces seeds, and how new plants grow out of these, he will find the supersensible form of energy especially powerful, when he observes these seeds. At this period the physical being is insignificant in a certain respect, whereas the supersensible entity is highly differentiated and contains everything that, from the supersensible world, contributes to the growth of the plant.

Now in the same way by supersensible observation of the whole earth, we discover an entity of force which we can know with absolute certainty existed before everything came into being which is perceptible by the senses upon and within the earth. In this way we arrive at an experience of the presence of those supersensible forces which co-operated in forming and developing the earth in the past. What is thus experienced we may just as well call the etheric or elemental basic entities or bodies of the plant and of the earth, as we call the body through which we gain perception when outside the body, our own elemental or etheric body.

Even when we first begin to be able to observe in a supersensible way, we can assign elemental basic-entities of this kind to certain things and processes apart from their ordinary qualities, which are perceptible in the world of the senses. We are able to speak of an etheric body belonging to the plant or to the earth. However, the elemental beings observed in this way are not by any means the only ones which reveal themselves to supersensible experience. We characterise the elemental body of a plant by saying that it builds up a form from the materials and forces of the physical world and thereby manifests its life in a physical body. But we may also observe beings that lead an elemental existence without manifesting their life in a physical body. Thus entities that are purely elemental are revealed to supersensible observation. It is not merely that we experience an addition, as it were, to the physical world; we experience another world in which the world of the senses presents itself as something which may be compared to pieces of ice floating about in water. A man who could only see the ice and not the water might quite possibly ascribe reality to the ice only and not to the water. Similarly, if we take into account only that which manifests itself to the senses, we may deny the existence of the supersensible world, of which the world of the senses is in reality a part, just as the floating pieces of ice are part of the water in which they are floating.

Now we shall find that those who are able to make supersensible observations describe what they behold by making use of expressions borrowed from the perceptions of sense. Thus we may find the elemental body of a being in the world of the senses, or that of a purely elemental being, described as manifesting itself as a self-contained body of light and having manifold colours. These colours flash forth, glow or shine, and it appears that these phenomena of light and colour are the manifestation of its life. But that of which the observer is really speaking is altogether invisible, and he is perfectly aware that the light or colour-picture which he gives, has no more to do with that which he actually perceives than, for instance, the writing in which a fact is communicated has to do with the fact itself. And yet the supersensible experience has not been expressed through arbitrarily chosen perceptions of the senses. The picture seen is actually before the observer, and is similar to an impression of the senses. This is so because, during supersensible experiences liberation from the physical body is not complete. The physical body is still connected with the elemental body, and brings the supersensible experience in a form drawn from the sense world. Thus the description given of an elemental being is given in the form of a visionary or fanciful combination of sense-impressions. But in spite of this, it is, when given in this manner, a true rendering of what has been experienced. For we have really seen what we are describing. The mistake that may be made is not in describing the vision as such, but in taking the vision for the reality, instead of that to which the vision points namely, the reality underlying it. A man who has never seen colours - a man born blind - will not, when he attains to the corresponding faculty of perception, describe elemental beings in such a way as to speak of flashing colours. He will make use of expressions familiar to him. To people, however, who are able to see physically, it is quite appropriate when they, in their description, make use of some such expression as the flashing forth of a colour form. By its aid they can give an impression of what has been seen by the observer of the elemental world. And this holds good not only for communications made by a clairvoyant - that is to say, one who is able to perceive by the aid of his elemental body - to a non-clairvoyant, but also for the intercommunication between

   A Road To Self-Knowledge

clairvoyants themselves. In the world of the senses man lives in his physical body, and this body clothes the supersensible observations in forms perceptible to the senses. Therefore the expression of supersensible observations by making use of the sense- pictures they produce is, in ordinary earth-life, a useful means of communication.

The point is, that any one receiving communication experiences in his soul something bearing the right relation to the fact in question. Indeed, the pictures are only communicated in order to call forth an experience. Such as they really are, they cannot be found in the outer world. That is their characteristic and also the reason why they call forth experiences that have no relation to anything material.

At the beginning of his clairvoyance, the pupil will find it difficult to become independent of the sense picture. When his faculty becomes more developed, however, a craving will arise for inventing more arbitrary means of communicating what has been seen. These will involve the necessity for explaining the signs which he uses. The more the exigencies of our time demand the general diffusion of supersensible knowledge, the greater will be the necessity for clothing such knowledge in the expressions used in everyday life on the physical plane.

Now at certain times supersensible experiences may come upon the pupil of themselves. And he has then the opportunity of learning something about the supersensible world by personal experience according as he is more or less often favoured, as we may say, by that world through its shining into the ordinary life of his soul. A higher faculty however is that of calling forth at will clairvoyant perception from the soul-life. The path to the attainment of this faculty results ordinarily from energetic continuation of the inner strengthening of the soul-life, but much also depends upon establishing a certain keynote in the soul. A calm unruffled attitude of mind is necessary in regard to the supersensible world - an attitude which is as far removed on the one hand from the burning desire to experience the most possible in the clearest possible manner as it is from a personal lack of interest in that world. Burning desire has the effect of diffusing something like an invisible mist before the clairvoyant sight, whilst lack of interest acts in such a way that though the supersensible facts really do manifest themselves, they are simply not noticed. This lack of interest shows itself now and then in a very peculiar form. There are persons who honestly wish for supersensible experiences, but they form a priori a certain definite idea of what these experiences should be in order to be acknowledged as real. Then when the real experiences arrive, they flit by without being met by any interest, just because they are not such as one has imagined that they ought to be.

In the case of voluntarily produced clairvoyance there comes a moment in the course of the soul's inner activity when we know: now my soul is experiencing something that it never experienced before. The experience is not a definite one, but a general feeling that we are not confronting the outer world of the senses, nor are we within it, nor yet are we within ourselves as in the ordinary life of the soul. The outer and inner experiences melt into one, into a feeling of life, hitherto unknown to the soul, concerning which, however, the soul knows that it could not be felt if it were only living within the outer world by means of the senses or by its ordinary feelings and recollections. We feel, moreover, that during this condition of the soul something is penetrating into it from a world hitherto unknown. We cannot, however, arrive at a conception of this unknown something. We have the experience but can form no idea of it. Now we shall find that when we have such an experience we get a feeling as if there were a hindrance in our physical bodies preventing us from forming a conception of that which is penetrating into the soul. If, however, we continue the inner efforts of our soul we shall, after a while, feel that we have overcome our own corporeal resistance.

The physical apparatus of the intellect had hitherto only been able to form ideas in connection with experiences in the world of the senses. It is at the outset incapable of raising to a picture that which wants to manifest itself from out of the supersensible world. It must first be so prepared as to be able to do this. In the same way as a child is surrounded by the outer world, but has to have his intellectual apparatus prepared by experience in that world before he is able to form ideas of his surroundings, so is mankind in general unable to form an idea of the supersensible world. The clairvoyant who wishes to make progress prepares his own apparatus for forming ideas so that it will work on a higher level in exactly the same way as that of a child is prepared to work in the world of the senses. He makes his strengthened thoughts work upon this apparatus and as a consequence the latter is by degrees remodeled. He becomes capable of including the supersensible world in the realm of his ideas.

Thus we feel how through the activity of the soul we can influence and remodel our own body. In the beginning the body acts as a strong counterpoise to the life of the soul; we feel it as a foreign body within us. But presently we notice how it always adapts itself increasingly to the experiences of the soul; until, finally, we do not feel it any more at all, but find before us the supersensible world, just as we do not notice the existence of the eye with which we look upon the world of colours. The body then must become imperceptible before the soul can behold the supersensible world.

When we have in this way deliberately arrived at making the soul clairvoyant, we shall, as a rule, be able to reproduce this state at will if we concentrate upon some thought that we are able to experience within ourselves in a specially powerful manner. As a consequence of surrendering ourselves to such a thought we shall find that clairvoyance is brought about.

At first we shall not be able to see anything definite which we especially wish to see. Supersensible things or happenings for which we are in no way prepared, or desire to call forth, will play into the life of the soul. Yet, by continuing our inner efforts, we shall also attain to the faculty of directing the spiritual eye to such things as we wish to investigate. When we have forgotten an experience we try to being it back to our memory by recalling to the mind something connected with the experience; and in the same way we may, as clairvoyants, start from an experience which we may rightly think is connected with what we want to find. In surrendering ourselves with intensity to the known experience, we shall often after a longer or shorter lapse of time find added to it that experience which it was our object to attain. In general, however, it is to be noted that it is of the very greatest importance for the clairvoyant quietly to wait for the propitious moment. We should not desire to attract anything. If a desired experience does not arrive, it is best to give up the search for a while and to try to get an opportunity another time. The human apparatus of cognition needs to develop calmly up to the level of certain experiences. If we have not the patience to await such development, we shall make incorrect or inaccurate observations.

FOURTH MEDITATION

In which the Attempt is made to form a Conception of the Guardian of the Threshold

WHEN the soul has attained the faculty of making observations whilst remaining outside the physical body, certain difficulties may arise with regard to its emotional life. It may find itself compelled to take up quite a different position towards itself from that to which it was formerly accustomed. The soul was accustomed to regard the physical world as outside itself, while it considered all inner experience as its own particular possession. To supersensible surroundings, however, it cannot take up the same position as to the outer world. As soon as the soul perceives the supersensible world around it, it must merge with it to a certain extent: it cannot consider itself as separate from these surroundings as it does from the outer world. Through this fact all that can be designated as our own inner world in relation to the supersensible surroundings assumes a certain character which is not easily reconcilable with the idea of inward privacy. We can no longer say, "I think, " " I feel, " or "I have my thoughts and fashion them as I like." But we must say instead, " Something thinks in me, something makes emotions flash forth in me, something forms thoughts and compels them to come forward in an absolutely definite way and make their presence felt in my consciousness."

Now this feeling may contain something exceedingly depressing when the manner in which the supersensible experience presents itself is such as to convey the certainty that we are actually experiencing a reality and are not losing ourselves in imaginary fancies or illusions. Such as it is it may indicate that the supersensible surrounding world wants to feel, and to think for itself, but that it is hindered in the realisation of its intention. At the same time we get a feeling that that which here wants to enter the soul is the true reality and the only one that can give an explanation of all we have hitherto experienced as real. This feeling also gives the impression that the supersensible reality shows itself as something which in value infinitely transcends the reality hitherto known to the soul. This feeling is therefore depressing, because it makes us feel that we are actually forced to will the next step which has to be taken. It lies in the very nature of that which we have become through our own inner experience to take this step. If we do not take it we must feel this to be a denial of our own being, or even self- annihilation. And yet we may also have the feeling that we cannot take it, or if we attempt it as far as we can, it must remain imperfect

All this develops into the idea: Such as the soul now is, a task lies before it, which it cannot master, because such as it now is, it is rejected by its supersensible surroundings, for the supersensible world does not wish to have it within its realm. And so the soul arrives at a feeling of being in contradiction to the supersensible world; and has to say to itself: "I am not such as to make it possible for me to mingle with that world, and yet only there can I learn the true reality and my relation to it; for I have separated myself from the recognition of Truth." This feeling means an experience which will make more and more clear and decisive the exact value of our own soul. We feel ourselves and our whole life to be steeped in an error.

And yet this error is distinct from other errors. The others are thought; but this is a living experience. An error that is only thought may be removed when the wrong thought is replaced by the right one. But the error that has been experienced has become part of the life of our soul itself; we ourselves are the error, we cannot simply correct it, for, think as we will, it is there, it is part of reality, and that, too, our own reality. Such an experience is a crushing one for the "self." We feel our inmost being painfully rejected by all that we desire. This pain, which is felt at a certain stage in the pilgrimage of the soul, is far beyond anything which can be felt as pain in the physical world. And therefore it may surpass everything which we have hitherto become able to master in the life of our soul. It may have the effect of stunning us. The soul stands before the anxious question: Whence shall I gather strength to carry the burden laid upon me? And the soul must find that strength within its own life. It consists in something that may be characterised as inner courage, inner fearlessness.

In order now to be able to proceed further in the pilgrimage of the soul, we must have developed so far that the strength which enables us to bear our experiences will well up from within us and produce this inner courage and inner fearlessness in a degree never required for life in the physical body.

Such strength is only produced by true self-knowledge. In fact it is only at this stage of development that we realise how little we have hitherto really known of ourselves. We have surrendered ourselves to our inner experiences without observing them as one observes a part of the outer world. Through the steps that have led to the faculty of extra-physical experience, however, we obtain a special means of self-knowledge. We learn in a certain sense to contemplate ourselves from a standpoint which can only be found when we are outside the physical body. And the depressing feeling mentioned before is itself the very beginning of true self-knowledge. To realise oneself as being in error in one's relations to the outer world is a sign that one is realising the true nature of one's own soul.

It is in the nature of the human soul to feel such enlightenment regarding itself as painful. It is only when we feel this pain that we learn how strong is the natural desire to feel ourselves, just as we are - to be human beings of importance and value. It may seem an ugly fact that this is so; but we have to face this ugliness of our own self without prejudice. We did not notice it before, just because we never consciously penetrated deeply enough into our own being. Only when we do so do we perceive how dearly we love that in ourselves which must be felt as ugly. The power of self-love shows itself in all its enormity. And at the same time we see how little inclination we have to lay aside this self-love. Even when it is only a question of those qualities of the soul which are concerned with our ordinary life and relations to other people, the difficulties turn out to be quite great enough. We learn, for instance, by means of true self-knowledge, that though we have hitherto believed that we felt kindly towards some one, nevertheless we are cherishing in the depths of our soul secret envy or hatred or some such feeling towards that person. We realise that these feelings, which have not as yet risen to the surface, will some day certainly crave for expression. And we see how very superficial it would be to say to ourselves: "Now that you have learned how it stands with you, root out your envy or hatred." For we discover that armed merely with such a thought we shall certainly feel exceedingly weak, when some day the craving to show our envy or to satisfy our hatred breaks forth as if with elemental power. Such special kinds of self-knowledge manifest themselves in different people according to the special constitution of their souls. They appear when experience outside the body begins, for then our self-knowledge becomes a true one, and is no longer troubled by any desire to find ourselves modeled in some such way as we should like to be.

Such special self-knowledge is painful and depressing to the soul, but if we want to attain to the faculty of experience outside the body, it cannot be avoided, for it is necessarily called forth by the special position which we must take up with regard to our own soul. For the very strongest powers of the soul are required, even if it is only a question of an ordinary human being obtaining self-knowledge in a general way. We are observing ourselves from a standpoint outside our previous inner life.

We have to say to ourselves: "I have contemplated and judged the things and occurrences of the world according to my human nature. I must now try to imagine that I cannot contemplate and judge them in that way. But then I should not be what I am. I should have no inner experiences. I should be a mere nothing." And not only a man in the midst of ordinary everyday life, who only very rarely even thinks about the world or life, would have to address himself in this way. Any man of science, or any philosopher, would have to do so. For even philosophy is only observation and judgment of the world according to individual qualities and conditions of the human soul-life. Now such a judgment cannot mingle with supersensible surroundings. It is rejected by them. And therewith everything we have been up to that moment is rejected. We look back upon our whole soul, upon our ego itself, as upon something which has to be laid aside, when we want to enter the supersensible world. The soul, however, cannot but consider this ego as its real being until it enters the supersensible worlds. The soul must consider it as the true human being, and must say to itself: "Through this my ego I have to form ideas of the world. I must not lose this ego of mine if I do not want to give myself up as a being altogether.' There is in the soul the strongest inclination to guard the ego at all points in order not to lose one's foothold absolutely. What the soul thus feels of necessity to be right in ordinary life, it must no longer feel when it enters supersensible surroundings. It has there to cross a threshold, where it must leave behind not only this or that precious possession, but that very being which it has hitherto believed itself to be. The soul must be able to say to itself: "That which until now has seemed to me to be my surest truth, I must now, on the other side of the threshold of the supersensible world, be able to consider as my deepest error."

Before such a demand the soul may well recoil. The feeling may be so strong that the necessary steps would seem a surrender of its own being, and an acknowledgment of its own nothingness, so that it admits more or less completely on the threshold its own powerlessness to fulfil the demands put before it. This acknowledgment may take all possible forms. It may appear merely as an instinct and seem to the pupil who thinks and acts upon it as something quite different from what it really is. He may, for instance, feel a great dislike to all supersensible truths. He may consider them as day dreams, or imaginary fancies. He does so only because in those depths of his soul of which he is ignorant he has a secret fear of these truths. He feels that he can only live with that which is admitted by his senses and his intellectual judgment. He therefore avoids arriving at the threshold of the supersensible world, and he veils the fact of his avoidance of it by saying: " That which is supposed to lie behind that threshold is not tenable by reason or by science." The fact is simply that he loves reason and science such as he knows them, because they are bound up with his ego. This is a very, frequent form of self-love and cannot as such be brought into the supersensible world.

It may also happen that there is not only this instinctive halt before the threshold. The pupil may consciously proceed to the threshold and then turn back, because he fears that which lies before him. He will then not easily be able to blot out from the ordinary life of his soul the effect of thus approaching it. The effect will be that weakness will spread over the whole of his soul's life.

What ought to take place is this, that the pupil on entering the supersensible world should make himself able to renounce that which in ordinary life he considers as the deepest truth and to adapt himself to a different way of feeling and judging

 A Road To Self-Knowledge

things. But at the same time he must keep in mind that when he again confronts the physical world, he must make use of the ways of feeling, and judging that are suitable for this physical world. He must not only learn to live in two different worlds, but also to live in each in quite a different way, and he must not allow his sound judgment, which he needs for ordinary life in the world of reason and of the senses, to be encroached upon by the fact that he is obliged to make use of another kind of discernment while in another world.

To take up such a position is difficult for human nature, and the capacity for doing so is only acquired through continued energetic and patient strengthening of our soul-life. Any one who goes through the experiences of the threshold realises that it is a boon to the ordinary life of the soul not to be led so far. The feelings that awaken are such that one cannot but think that this boon proceeds from some powerful entity, who protects man from the danger of undergoing the dread of self-annihilation at the threshold.

Behind the outer world of ordinary life there is another. Before the threshold of this world a stern guardian is standing, who prevents man from knowing what the laws of the supersensible world are. For all doubts and all uncertainty concerning that world are, after all, easier to bear than the sight of that which one must leave behind when we want to cross the threshold.

The pupil remains protected against the experience described, as long as he does not step forward to the very threshold. The fact that he receives descriptions of such experiences from those who have trodden or crossed this threshold does not change the fact of his being protected. On the contrary, such communications may be of good service to him when he approaches the threshold. In this case as in many others, a thing is done better if one has an idea of it beforehand. But as regards the self-knowledge which must be gained by a traveler in the supersensible world nothing is changed by such preliminary knowledge. It is therefore not in harmony with the facts, when many clairvoyants, or those acquainted with the nature of clairvoyance, assert that these things should not be mentioned at all to people who are not on the point of resolving to enter into the supersensible world. We are now living in a time when people must become more and more acquainted with the nature of the supersensible world, if the life of their soul is to become equal to the demands of ordinary life upon it. The spread of supersensible knowledge, including the knowledge of the guardian of the threshold, is one of the tasks of the moment and of the immediate future.

A Road To Self-Knowledge

FIFTH MEDITATION

In which the Attempt is made to form an Idea of the Astral Body WHEN we experience through our elemental body a surrounding supersensible world, we feel ourselves less separated from that world than we are from physical surroundings when in our physical body. And yet we bear a relation to these supersensible surroundings, which may be expressed by saying that we have attached to ourselves certain substances of the elemental world in the form of an elemental body, just as in the physical outer world we carry some of its materials and forces attached to us in the shape of our physical body. We observe that this is so when we want to find our way about in the supersensible world outside the physical body. It may happen that we have before us some fact or being of the supersensible world. It may be there, and we can behold it, but we do not know what it is. If we are strong enough, we may drive it away, but only by carrying ourselves back into the world of the senses by energetic concentration upon our experiences in that world. We are, however, unable to remain in the supersensible world and compare with other beings or facts the being or the fact perceived. And yet it is only by so doing that we could form a correct estimate of what is beheld. Thus our "sight" in the supersensible world may be limited to the perception of single things without the faculty of moving freely from one thing to another. We then feel fettered to that single thing.

We may now look for the reason of this limitation. This can only be found when through further inner development the life of our soul has been still more strengthened and we arrive at a point when this limitation is no longer there. And then we shall discover that the reason why we could not move from one thing to another is to be found in our own soul. We learn that sight in the supersensible world differs in this way from perception in the world of the senses. One can, for instance, in the physical world see every visible thing when one has got sound eyes. If one sees one thing one can also, with the same eyes, see all other things. This is not so in the supersensible world.

One can have the organ of supersensible perception developed in such a way that one can experience this or that fact, but if another fact is to be perceived one's organ must first be specially developed for this purpose. Such a development gives one the feeling that an organ has awoke to a particular region of the supersensible world. One feels as if one's elemental body were in a kind of sleep with regard to the supersensible world, and as if it had to be awoke with regard to each particular thing. It is in fact possible to speak of being asleep and being awake in the elemental world; but they are not alternate states as in the physical world. They are states existing in man simultaneously. As long as we have not attained any faculty for experience through our elemental body, that body is asleep. We always carry this body about with us, but it is a sleeping body. With the strengthening of the life of our soul the awakening begins, but at first only for a part of the elemental body. The more we awaken our elemental being, ' the deeper we penetrate into the elemental world.

In the elemental world itself there is nothing that can aid the soul to bring about this awakening. However much may be beheld, one thing perceived adds nothing to the possibility of perceiving another thing. Free movement in the supersensible world can be attained by the soul through nothing that is found in the elemental environment. When we continue the exercises to strengthen the soul, we attain more and more this power of moving in particular regions. Through all this our attention is

A Road To Self-Knowledge

drawn to something in ourselves, which does not belong to the elemental world, but is discovered within ourselves through our experience of that world. We feel ourselves as particular beings in the supersensible world, who seem to be the rulers, directors, and masters of their elemental bodies, and who by and by awaken these bodies to supersensible consciousness.

When we have arrived so far, a feeling of intense loneliness overwhelms the soul. We find ourselves in a world that is elemental in all directions; we see only ourselves within endless elemental space as beings which can nowhere find their equal. It is not affirmed that every development to clairvoyance should lead to this fearful loneliness, but any one who consciously and by his own efforts acquires a strengthening of his soul, will meet with it. And if he follow a teacher who gives him directions from step to step in order to further his development, he will, perhaps late, but still some day, have to realise that his teacher has left him all to himself. He will find that his teacher has left him, and that he is abandoned to loneliness in the elemental world. Only afterwards will he understand that he has been obliged to let him depend upon himself since the necessity for such self-reliance had asserted itself.

At this stage of the soul's pilgrimage the pupil feels himself an exile in the elemental world. But now he can go on further if sufficient force has been aroused in him through his inner exercises. He may begin to see a new world emerge - not in the elemental world, but within himself - a world that is not one either with the physical or with the elemental world. For such a pupil a second supersensible world is added to the first. This second supersensible world is at first completely an inner world. The pupil feels that he carries it within himself and that he is alone with it. To compare this state to anything in the world of the senses, let us take the following case. Somebody has lost all his dear ones through death and now carries only the recollection of them in his soul. They live on for him only as his thoughts. Thus it is in the second supersensible world. Man stands to this second supersensible world in such a way that he carries it within himself; but he knows that he is shut out from its reality. Nevertheless he feels that this reality within his soul, whatever it may be, is something much more real than mere recollection from the world of the senses. This supersensible world lives an independent life within one's own soul. All that is there is yearning to get out of the soul, and arrive at something else. Thus one feels a world within oneself, but a world that does not want to remain there. This produces a feeling like being torn asunder by every separate detail of that world. One may arrive at a point where these details free themselves, where they break through something which seems like a shell and escape from the soul. Then one may feel oneself the poorer by all that has in this manner torn itself away from the soul.

One now learns that that part of the supersensible reality in the soul which one is able to love for its own sake, and not simply because it is actually in one's own soul, behaves in a particular way. What one can thus love deeply does not tear itself from the soul; it certainly does force its way out of the soul, but carries the soul along with it. It carries the soul to that region where it lives in its true reality. A kind of union with the real essence takes place, for hitherto one has only carried something like a reflection of this real essence within one. The love here mentioned must, however, be of the kind that is experienced in the supersensible world. In the world of the senses one can only prepare oneself for such love. And this preparation takes place when one strengthens one's capacity for love in the world of the senses. The greater the love of which one is capable in the physical world, the more of this capacity remains for the supersensible world. With regard to the individual entities of the supersensible world, this works as follows.

You cannot, for instance, get into touch with those real

supersensible beings which are connected with the plants of the physical world if you do not love plants in the world of the senses, and so on. An error, however, may very easily arise with regard to such things. It may happen that somebody in the physical world passes the vegetable kingdom by with complete indifference, and yet an unconscious affinity for that kingdom may lie hidden in the soul.

Afterwards when he enters the supersensible world this love may awaken.

But the union with beings in the supersensible world does not only depend upon love. Other feelings, as, for instance, respect and reverence, which the soul may have for a being when it first feels the picture of this being arise within it, have the same effect. These qualities will, however, always be such as must be reckoned as belonging to the inner qualities of the soul. One will in this way learn to know those beings of the supersensible world to which the soul itself opened the way through such inner qualities. A sure way to get acquainted with the supersensible world consists in gaining access to the different beings through one's relationship to their reflections. In the world of the senses we love a being after having learned to know him; in the second supersensible world we may love the image of a being before meeting with the being itself, as this image presents itself before the meeting takes place.

That which the soul in this way learns to know within itself is not the elemental body. It stands in relation to that body as its "awakener." It is a being dwelling within the soul which is experienced in the same way as that in which you would experience yourself during sleep if you were not unconscious but felt yourself to be conscious when outside your physical body and in the position of its " awakener " at the moment of its rousing from sleep. Thus the soul learns to know a being within itself which is a third something beside the physical and the elemental bodies. Let us call this something the astral body, and this expression shall, for the time being, mean nothing but that which in the way described is experienced within the being of the soul.

SIXTH MEDITATION

In which the Attempt is made to form a Conception of the Ego-Body or Thought-Body

THE feeling of being outside our physical body is stronger during experiences within the astral body than during those within the elemental body. In the case of the elemental body we feel ourselves outside the region in which the physical body exists, and yet we feel connected with the latter body. In the astral body we feel the physical body itself as something outside our own being. On passing into the elemental body we feel something like an expansion of our own being; but in identifying our consciousness with the astral body it is as though we made a jump into another being. And we feel a world of spiritual beings sending their activities into that being. We feel ourselves in some way or other connected with or related to these beings. And by degrees we learn to know how these beings are mutually connected. To our human consciousness the world widens out in the direction of the spiritual. We behold spiritual beings, for example, who bring about the succession of epochs in the development of mankind so that we realise that the different characters of the different epochs are, as it were, stamped upon them by real spiritual entities. These are the Spirits of Time or Primordial Powers (Archai). We learn to know other beings, whose psychic life is such that their thoughts are at the same time active forces of nature. We are led to understand that only to physical perception do the forces of nature appear to be constituted as physical perception imagines them to be. That in fact everywhere, where a force of nature is acting, the thought of some being is expressing itself just as a human soul finds expression in the movement of a hand. All this is not as though man by the aid of any theory is able in thought to place living beings at the back of nature's processes; when we realise ourselves in our astral body we enter into quite as concrete and real a relation to those beings as that between human individuals in the physical world. Among the spirits into whose realm we thus penetrate we discover a series of gradations, and we may thus speak of a world of higher hierarchies. Those beings whose thoughts manifest themselves to physical perception as forces of nature we may call Spirits of Form.

Experience in that world assumes that we feel our physical being as something outside us, in the same way as in physical existence we look upon a plant as a thing outside ourselves. We shall feel this state of being outside all that in ordinary life must be felt as the whole compass of our own being, as a very painful one, so long as it is not accompanied by a certain other experience. If the inner work of the soul has been energetically carried on and has led to a proper deepening and strengthening of the life of our soul, it is not necessary that this pain should be very pronounced. For a slow and gradual entrance into that second experience may be accomplished simultaneously with our entrance into the astral body as our natural vehicle.

This second experience will consist in obtaining the capacity for considering all that, which before filled and was connected with our own soul, as a kind of recollection, so that we stand in the same relation to our own former ego as we do to our recollections in the physical world. Only through such an experience do we attain to full consciousness of ourselves as truly living with our own real being in a world quite different from that of the senses.

We now possess the knowledge that that which we carry about with us and have hitherto considered as our ego is something different from what we really are. We are now able to stand opposite to ourselves, and we may form an idea concerning that which now confronts our own soul and of which it formerly said, "That is myself." Now the soul no longer says, "That is myself," but, " I am carrying that something about with me." Just as the ego in ordinary life feels independent of its own recollections, so our newly- found ego feels itself independent of our former ego. It feels that it belongs to a world of purely spiritual beings. And as this experience - a real experience: no mere theory - comes to us, so we realise what that really is which we hitherto considered as our ego. It presents itself as a web of recollections, produced by the physical, the elemental, and the astral bodies in the same way as an image is produced by a mirror. Just as little as a man identifies himself with his rejected picture, so little does the soul, experiencing itself in the spiritual world, identify itself with that which it experiences of itself in the world of the senses. The comparison with the rejected image is, of course, to be taken merely as a comparison.

For the reflected image vanishes when we change our position with regard to the mirror. The web woven of recollections and representing what we in the physical world consider as our own being, has a greater degree of independence than the image in the mirror. It has in a certain way a being of its own. And yet to the real being of the soul it is only like a picture of our real self. The real being of the soul feels that this picture is needed for the manifestation of its real self. This real being knows that it is something different, but also that it would never have attained to any real knowledge of itself if it had not at first realised itself as its own image within that world, which, after its ascent into the spiritual world, becomes an outer world.

The web of recollection which we now regard as our former ego may be called the "ego-body" or "thought-body." The word "body" must in this connection be taken in a wider sense than that which is usually called a "body." By "body " is here meant all that we experience as belonging to us and of which we do not say, "We are it," but, "We possess it."

Only when clairvoyant consciousness has arrived at the point where it experiences, as a sum of recollections, that which it formerly considered to be itself, does it become possible to acquire real experience of what is hidden behind the phenomenon of death. For then we have arrived at a truly real world in which we feel ourselves as beings who are able to retain, as though in a memory, what has been experienced in the world of the senses. This sum total of experiences in the physical world needs - in order to continue its existence - a being who is able to retain it in the same way in which the ordinary ego retains its recollections. Supersensible knowledge discloses that man has an existence within the world of spiritual beings, and that it is he himself who keeps within him his physical existence as a recollection. The question what after death will become of all that I now am, receives the following answer from clairvoyant investigation: "You will continue to be yourself just to that extent to which you realise that self to be a spiritual being amongst other spiritual beings."

We realise the nature of these spiritual beings and amongst them our own nature. And this knowledge is direct experience. Through it we know that spiritual beings, and with them our own soul, have an existence of which the physical existence is but a passing manifestation. If to ordinary consciousness it appears - as shown in the First Meditation - that the body belongs to a world whose real part in it is proved by its dissolution therein after death, clairvoyant observation teaches us that the real human ego belongs to a world to which it is attached by bonds quite different from those which connect the body with the laws of nature. The bonds which attach the ego to the spiritual beings of the supersensible world are not touched in their innermost character either by birth or by death. In physical existence these bonds only show themselves in a special way. That which appears in this world is the expression of realities of a supersensible nature. Now as man as such is a supersensible being, and also appears so to supersensible observation, so the bonds between souls in the supersensible world are not affected by death. And that anxious question which comes before the ordinary consciousness of the soul in this primitive form: " Shall I meet again after death those with whom I know I have been connected during physical existence?" must, by any real investigator, who is entitled to form a judgment based upon experience, be emphatically answered in the affirmative.

Everything that has been said of the being of the soul experiencing itself as a spiritual reality within the world of other spiritual beings, may be seen and confirmed if we strengthen the life of our soul in the way mentioned before. And it is possible to make this easier and to help oneself along by the development of special feelings. In ordinary life in the physical world we take up such a position to all that we feel to be our fate, as to feel sympathy or antipathy for different occurrences. A self-observer, who is able to remain quite unbiased, must admit that these sympathies and antipathies are some of the strongest that man is able to feel. Ordinary reflection upon the fact that everything in life is a result of necessity, and that we have to bear our fate, may certainly take us a long way towards a deliberate attitude of mind in life. But in order to be able to grasp something of the real being of man still more is required. The reflection described will do excellent service in the life of our soul. We may, however, often find that those sympathies and antipathies of the kind mentioned, which we have been able to discard, have only disappeared from our immediate consciousness. They have retired into the deeper strata of human nature and manifest themselves as a certain mood of the soul or as a feeling of slackness or some other such sensation in the body. Real imperturbability with regard to fate is only acquired when we behave in this matter in just the same way as in the repeated concentrated surrender to thoughts or feelings for the purpose of strengthening the soul in general. A reflection only leading to intellectual understanding is not sufficient. It is necessary to live intensely with such a reflection, and to continue in it for a certain period of time while keeping away all experiences appertaining to the senses or other recollections of ordinary life. Through such exercises we arrive at a certain fundamental attitude of mind towards fate. It is possible radically to do away with sympathies and antipathies in this respect and finally to consider everything that happens to us quite as unconcernedly as an observer watches water falling over a mountainside and splashing down beneath. It is not meant that in this way we ought to arrive at facing our own fate without any feelings whatever. One who becomes indifferent to anything that happens to him is surely on no profitable track. We certainly do not remain indifferent to the outer world with regard to things not touching our own soul as part of our fate. We look upon things happening before our eyes with pleasure or with pain.

Indifference to life should not be sought, when we strive after supersensible knowledge, but transformation of the direct interest that the ego takes in its own fate. It is quite possible that by such transformation the vividness of the life of feeling is strengthened and not weakened. In ordinary life tears are shed over many things that happen to our own soul in the way of fate.

We are, however, able to win our way to a standpoint where the unfortunate fate of others awakens in our soul the same keen interest and feeling as are induced by our own unhappy experiences. It is easier to arrive at such a standpoint with regard to misfortunes that fate brings us than, for example, with regard to our mental capacities. It is not so easy, after all, to experience as great a joy when you discover a capacity in another, as when you discover that you possess that capacity yourself. When self-observation strives to penetrate into the

                                   A Road To Self-Knowledge

depths of the soul, much selfish satisfaction with many things which we can do ourselves may be discovered. An intense, repeated meditative union with the thought, that in many instances it is quite indifferent to the course of human life whether we ourselves or others are able to do certain things, may carry us a long way towards true imperturbability with regard to that which we feel to be the innermost working of fate in our own lives. Such inner reinforcement of the life of our soul, by steeping it in thought, when rightly done, can never lead to a mere blunting of our feeling for our own capacities. Instead they are transformed and we realise the necessity of behaving in accordance with these capacities.

And here we have already indicated the direction taken by this strengthening of the life of the soul by thought. We learn to realise something in ourselves which appears to the soul as a second being within it. This becomes especially manifest, when we connect with it thoughts which show how in ordinary life we bring about this or that event in our destiny. We are able to see that this or that would not have happened to us, if we had not behaved in a certain way at an earlier period in our life. What happens to us to-day is truly in many ways the result of what we did yesterday. We may now, with the intention of carrying our soul's experience further than some point at which we have arrived, look back upon our past experience. We may then search out all that shows how we ourselves have prepared our later destinies. We may try in so doing to go back so far as to reach that point where the consciousness awakens in the child, which enables it later in life to remember what it has experienced. If we set about this retrospect in such a way that we combine with it an attitude of mind which eliminates the usual selfish sympathies and antipathies with regard to occurrences in our own destiny, then, having reached in memory the above-mentioned point in our childhood, we face ourselves in such a way as to be able to say: At that time the possibility of feeling ourselves in ourselves and of conscious work upon the life of our soul first presented itself; but this ego of ours was there before, and it, although not working consciously within us, has brought us our capacity for knowledge as well as everything we now know. The attitude towards our own destiny just described brings about what no intellectual reflection is able to produce. We learn to look at the events of destiny with equanimity; we meet them with an unprejudiced mind; but we see in the being who brings these happenings upon us our own self. And when we look upon ourselves in this way, we find that the conditions of our own destiny, already given us at birth, are connected with our own self. We win our way to the conviction that just as we have worked upon ourselves since the awakening of our consciousness, so we had already been working before our present consciousness awoke. Now such a working of ourselves up to the realisation of a higher ego-being within the ordinary ego leads us not only to admit that our thoughts have brought us to a theoretical statement of the existence of such a higher ego, but also makes us realise as a power within ourselves the living activity of this ego in all its reality and feel the ordinary ego as a creation of the other. This feeling is, in fact, the first step towards beholding the spiritual being of the soul.

And if it leads to nothing, it is because we rest satisfied with the beginning only. This beginning may be a scarcely perceptible dull sensation. It may remain so perhaps for a long time. But if we strongly and energetically pursue the course which has led us up to this beginning, we shall at last arrive at beholding the soul as a spiritual being. And having brought ourselves thus far we shall easily understand why some one, without any experience in these matters, may say that in believing we see such things we have only created an imaginative picture of a higher ego through auto- suggestion. But one who has had the experience knows that such an objection can only be derived from lack of this very experience. For those who seriously go through this development acquire at the same time the capacity to distinguish between realities and the pictures of their own imagination. The inner activities and experiences which are necessary during such a pilgrimage of the soul, if it is a right one, make us practise the greatest circumspection towards ourselves with regard to imagination and reality. When we systematically strive to attain the experience of ourselves in the higher ego as spiritual beings, we shall consider as the principal experience that which is described at the beginning of this meditation and look upon the rest as a help to the soul on its pilgrimage.

SEVENTH MEDITATION

In which the Attempt is made to form an Idea of the Character of Experience in Supersensible Worlds

THE experiences that showed themselves to be necessary for the soul, if it wants to penetrate into supersensible worlds, may seem deterrent to many people. These may say they do not know what would befall them if they ventured upon such processes, or how they would be able to stand them.

Under the influence of such a feeling the opinion is very easily formed that it is better not to interfere artificially with the development of the soul, but calmly to surrender to the guidance of which the soul remains unconscious, and to await its effect in the future upon one's inner life. Such a thought must, however, always be repressed by a person who is able to make another thought a living power within him; namely, that it is natural to human nature to progress, and that if no attention were paid to these things it would mean disloyally consigning to stagnation forces in the soul which are waiting to be unfolded. Forces of self-unfolding are present in every human soul, and there cannot be a single one that would not listen to the call for unfolding them if in some way or other it could learn something about these powers and their importance.

Moreover, nobody will allow himself to be deterred from the ascent into higher worlds unless beforehand he has taken up a false position towards the processes through which he has to go. These processes are described in the preceding meditations. And if they are to be expressed by words which must naturally be taken from ordinary human existence, they can be rightly expressed only in that way. For experiences on the supersensible path of knowledge are related to the human soul in such a way that they are exactly similar to what, for example, a highly-strung feeling of loneliness, a feeling of hovering over an abyss and the like may mean to the soul of man.

Through the experience of such feelings and sensations the powers to tread the path of knowledge are produced. They are the germs of the fruits of supersensible knowledge. All these experiences in a certain way carry something in themselves which lies hidden deep within them, When they are experienced this hidden element is brought to a state of the utmost tension, something bursts the feeling of loneliness, which surrounds this hidden " something " like a veil, and it then pushes forward into the soul's life as a means of knowledge.

One must, however, take into consideration that when the right path is entered upon, something else at once presents itself behind every such experience. When the one has occurred, the other cannot fail to appear. When anything has to be borne there is at once added the power to bear it steadfastly if. we will only reflect calmly on this power and also take time to notice that which wants to manifest itself in the soul. When something painful appears, and when at the same time there is a sure feeling in the soul that forces are to be found which will make the pain bearable and with which we are able to connect ourselves, we are then able to take up such a position towards experiences, which would be unbearable in the course of our ordinary life, so that we seem to be the spectator of ourselves in all such experiences. And thus people who, whilst on their way towards supersensible knowledge, pass through many a rise and fall of great waves of feeling, show nevertheless perfect equanimity in ordinary life. It is of course quite possible that experiences that are made within also react upon the state of mind in outer life in the physical world, so that for a time we do not come into harmony with ourselves and with life in the way which was possible before we entered upon the path of knowledge. We are then obliged to draw from that which has already been obtained within ourselves such forces as make it possible again to find the balance. And if the path of knowledge be rightly trod no situation can arise in which this would not be possible.

The best path of knowledge will always be the one that leads to the supersensible world through strengthening or condensing the life of the soul by means of concentration on inner meditations during which certain thoughts or feelings are retained in the mind. In this case it is not a question of experiencing a thought or an emotion as we do in order to find our way in the physical world, but the point is to live entirely with and within the thought or emotion, concentrating all the powers of our soul in it, so that it entirely fills the consciousness during the time of retirement within ourselves. We think, for instance, of a thought which has given to the soul a conviction of some kind; we at first leave on one side any power of conviction it may have, and only live with it and in it again and again so as to become one with it. It is not necessary that it should be a thought of things belonging to the higher worlds, although such a thought is more effective. For inner meditation we can even use a thought which pictures an ordinary experience. Fruitful for instance, are emotions which represent resolutions with regard to deeds of love, and which we kindle within ourselves to the highest degree of human warmth and sincere experience. Effective - especially where knowledge is concerned - are symbolic representations, gained from life, or accepted on the advice of such persons as are in a certain way experts in these matters, because they know the fruitfulness of the means employed from what they themselves have gained by them.

Through these meditations, that must become a habit, nay, a necessity of life, just as breathing is necessary for the life of the body, we shall concentrate the powers of the soul, and by concentrating strengthen them. Only we must succeed during the time of inner meditation in remaining in such a state that neither outer impressions of the senses nor any recollections of such play upon the soul.

Recollections also of all that we have experienced in ordinary life, all that gives pleasure or pain to the soul, must remain silent so that the soul may surrender itself exclusively to that which we ourselves determine shall occupy it. The capacities for supersensible knowledge grow legitimately only out of that which we have acquired in this way by inner meditations, the content and the form of which have been fixed by the power of our own soul. The important point is not the source whence we derive the object of the meditation; we may take it from an expert in these matters or from the literature of spiritual science; the important point is to make its substance an inner experience of our own life and not merely to choose it out from thoughts which may arise in our own soul, or from things which we feel inclined to consider as the best objects for meditation. Such an object has but little power, because the soul is already familiar with it and cannot consequently make the necessary effort in order to become one with it. It is in making this effort, however, that the effective means of acquiring the faculties for supersensible knowledge are to be found, and not in the mere fact of becoming one with the substance of the meditation as such.

We can also arrive at supersensible sight in other ways. People may arrive at fervent meditation and inner experience by reason of their whole constitution. And so they may be able to liberate powers for acquiring supersensible knowledge in their soul. Such powers may all of a sudden manifest themselves in souls which do not seem at all predetermined for such experiences. In the most varied ways the supersensible life of the soul may awaken; but we can only arrive at an experience of which we are the masters as we are the masters of ourselves in ordinary life, if we tread the path of knowledge here described.

Any other irruption of the supersensible world into the experiences of the soul will mean that such experiences enter in as it were forcibly, and the person in question will either lose himself in them, or lay himself open to every conceivable kind of deception with regard to their value, their true meaning, and their importance within the real supersensible world.

It is most important to keep in mind that on the path to supersensible knowledge the soul changes. It may be the case that in ordinary life in the physical world, we are not at all inclined to fall into any kind of illusion or deception, but that on entering the supersensible world we fall victims to such deceptions and illusions in the most credulous manner. It may also happen that in the physical world we have a very good and sound feeling for truth, and understand that we must not think only in such a way of a thing or an occurrence as to satisfy our own' egoism in order to judge it rightly; yet in spite of this we may arrive at seeing in the supersensible world only what pleases our egoism. We must remember how this egoism colours all that we behold. We are observing only that to which our egoism is directing its gaze in accordance with its own inclinations, though perhaps we may not realise that it is egoism which is directing our spiritual sight. And it is then quite natural that we should take what we see for truth. Protection against this can only be obtained if, on the path to supersensible knowledge through earnest self-observation, and through an energetic striving for clearer self-knowledge, we more and more develop our capacity to discern truly how much egoism is to be found in our own soul and where it is finding utterance. Only then we shall be able to emancipate ourselves by degrees from the leadership of this egoism if in our meditation we forcibly and relentlessly put before ourselves the possibility of our soul being in this or that respect under its domination.

It belongs to the unhampered mobility of the soul in higher worlds that it should make clear to itself in what a different

A Road To Self-Knowledge

manner certain qualities of the soul react upon the spiritual world from that in which they do in the physical world. This becomes especially evident when we direct our attention to the moral qualities of the soul. Within the physical world we distinguish between the laws of nature and those of morality. When we want to explain natural processes we cannot make use of moral ideas. We explain a poisonous plant according to natural law, and we do not condemn it morally for being poisonous. We clearly understand that, with regard to the animal kingdom, there can, at the most, be only a question of something resembling morality, and that a moral judgment in the strict sense could only disturb the main issue. It is in circumstances of human life that moral judgment about the worth of existence begins to be of importance. Man himself makes his own value dependent on this judgment, when he comes so far that he is able to judge himself impartially. Nobody, however, would dream of considering the laws of nature as identical with or even similar to moral laws, if he considers physical existence in the right way.

As soon as we enter the higher worlds this is changed. The more spiritual the worlds which we enter, the more do moral law and what may be termed natural law in these worlds coincide. In the physical world we know that we are speaking figuratively when we say of an evil deed that it burns in the soul. We know that natural fire is quite a different thing. But such a distinction does not exist in the supersensible worlds; for there hate and envy are forces acting in such a way that we may term their effects the "natural laws" of that world. Hate and envy have there the effect that the being who is hated or envied reacts upon the hater or envier in a consuming, extinguishing manner, so that processes of destruction are established which are hurtful to the spiritual being. Love acts in such a way in spiritual worlds that its effect is an irradiation of warmth that is productive and helpful. This can already be observed in the elemental body of man. Within the sense-world the hand that commits an immoral action must in its activity be explained according to natural law quite in the same way as a hand that serves morality. But certain elemental parts of man remain undeveloped, when no corresponding moral feelings exist. And we must account for the imperfect formation of elemental organs through imperfect moral qualities in the same way as natural processes are explained by natural law. On the other hand, we must never from the imperfect development of a physical organ draw the conclusion that the corresponding part of the elemental body must be imperfectly developed. We must always keep in mind that in the different worlds different kinds of law prevail. A person may have a physical organ imperfectly developed; but at the same time the corresponding elemental organ may be not only normally perfect, but more perfect to the same extent as the physical one is imperfect. In a significant way does the difference between the supersensible and the physical worlds present itself in all that is connected with ideas of beauty and ugliness. The way in which these ideas are employed in physical existence loses all significance as soon as we enter supersensible worlds. Beautiful, for instance - only that being can be called beautiful which succeeds in communicating all its inner experiences to the other beings of its world, so that they can take part in the totality of its experience. The capacity of manifesting all that lives within oneself, and of not having to hide away anything, might in higher worlds be called "beautiful." And in these worlds this conception of beauty completely coincides with that of unreserved sincerity, of honest manifestation of that which a being carries within itself. Similarly that being might be called ugly which does not want to show outwardly its own inner content, and which holds back its own experience and hides itself from other beings with regard to certain qualities. Such a being withdraws from its spiritual surroundings. This conception of ugliness coincides with that of insincere manifestation of oneself. To lie and to be ugly are realities which in the spiritual world are

A Road To Self-Knowledge

identical, so that a being which appears ugly is a deceitful being.

What are known in the physical world as desires and wishes also appear with quite a different significance in the spiritual world. Desires which in the physical world arise from the inner nature of the human soul do not exist in the spiritual world. What may be termed desires in that world are kindled by that which is seen outside the being in question. A being which must feel that it has not a certain quality, which, according to that being's nature, it should have, beholds another being endowed with that quality, Moreover it cannot help having this other being always before it. As in the physical world the eye naturally sees what is visible, so in the supersensible world the want of a quality always carries a being into the neighbourhood of another being endowed with the quality in question. And the sight of this other being becomes a continual reproach that acts as a real force, making the being, who is hampered with the fault, desirous of amending it. This is a quite different experience from a desire in the physical world; for in the spiritual world free will is not interfered with through such circumstances. A being may oppose itself to that which the sight of something else will call forth within it. It will then succeed by degrees in being taken away from its model.

The consequence, however, will be that the being who opposes itself to its model will bring itself into worlds where the conditions of existence will be worse than those would have been which were given to it in the world for which it was in a certain way predestined.

All this shows the soul that its world of conceptions must be transformed when entering supersensible realms. Ideas must be changed, widened, and blended with others if we want to describe the supersensible world correctly. That is the reason why descriptions of supersensible worlds given in terms of the physical world without any alteration or transformation are always unsatisfactory. We may realise that it is the outcome of a correct human feeling, when we use, within the physical world - more or less symbolically or even as immediately applicable - ideas which only become fully significant with regard to supersensible worlds. Thus we may really feel lying to be ugly, but compared with the character of this idea in the supersensible world, such a use of words in the physical world is only a reflection, resulting from the fact that all the different worlds are related to one another, and these relations are dimly felt and unconsciously perceived in the physical world. Yet we must remember that in the physical world a lie, which we feel as ugly, is not necessarily ugly in its outer appearance, and that it would be a confusion of ideas if we were to explain ugliness in physical nature as the outcome of lying. In the supersensible world, however, anything false, seen in its right light, impresses itself upon us as being ugly in appearance. Here again possible deceptions have to be taken into consideration and guarded against. The soul may meet a being in the supersensible world which may rightly be characterised as evil, although it manifests itself in a form that must be called beautiful if judged according to the idea of the beautiful that we bring with us from the physical world. in such a case we shall not be able to judge correctly before we have penetrated to the heart of the being in question. We shall then discover that the "beautiful" manifestation was only a mask which does not harmonise with the nature of the being, and then that which we thought to be beautiful - according to ideas borrowed from the physical world - impresses itself with particular force upon our mind as ugly. And as soon as this happens, the " evil " being will no more be able to deceive us with its "beauty." It must unveil itself to such a beholder in its true form, which can only be an imperfect expression of that which it is within. Such phenomena of the supersensible world make it especially evident how human conceptions must be transformed when we enter that world.

EIGHTH MEDITATION

In which the Attempt is made to form an Idea of the Way in which Man beholds his Repeated Earth-Lives

WE are not really entitled to speak of dangers during the pilgrimage of the soul through supersensible worlds, when this pilgrimage is undertaken in the right way. The method would not lead to its goal if amongst the psychic instructions given there were those which created dangers for the pupil. The goal is rather to make the soul strong, to concentrate its forces, so that man should become able to bear his soul's experiences, which he has to go through when he wants to see and understand other worlds than the physical. Moreover, an essential difference between the physical world and the supersensible worlds is that beholding, perceiving, and understanding are related to one another in quite a different way in the two worlds. When we hear about some part of the physical world, we have a certain right to feel that we can only arrive at a complete understanding of it through beholding and perceiving it. We do not believe we have understood a landscape or a picture until we have seen it. But the supersensible worlds can be thoroughly understood when with unbiased judgment we accept a correct description of them. In order to understand and to experience all the forces for the strengthening and fulfilment of life which belong to spiritual worlds, we only need the descriptions of those who are able to see. Real knowledge of those worlds at first hand can only be obtained by those who are able to investigate when outside their physical body. Descriptions of the spiritual worlds must always originate with the seers. But such knowledge of these worlds as is necessary to the life of the soul may be obtained through the understanding. And it is perfectly possible to be unable to look into supersensible worlds oneself and yet be able to understand them and their peculiarities, with an understanding for which the soul has under certain circumstances a perfect right to ask, and indeed must ask.

Therefore it is also possible that we should choose our means of meditation out of the store of conceptions which we have acquired concerning the spiritual worlds. Such a means of meditation is by far the best and the one which leads us most safely to the goal.

Although such a notion may seem very natural, it is, however, not correct to believe that knowledge of higher worlds obtained through the understanding before attaining to supersensible vision is an obstacle to the development of such vision. The contrary is in fact more correct, namely, that it is easier and safer to arrive at clairvoyance with some preliminary understanding than without. Whether we stop short at understanding only, or go on to strive after clairvoyance, depends upon the awakening or non- awakening of an inner craving for firsthand knowledge. If such a craving is there, we cannot but look for every opportunity to start on a real personal pilgrimage into supersensible worlds.

The wish for an understanding of the higher worlds will spread more and more amongst the people of our day; for close observation of human evolution shows that from now onward human souls are entering upon a stage of development in which they will be unable to find the right relation to life without an understanding of supersensible worlds.

* * * * *

When we have come so far on our soul's pilgrimage that we carry within ourselves as a memory all that we call "ourself," namely, our own being in physical life, and experience ourselves instead in another, newly-won superior ego, then we become capable of seeing our life stretching beyond the limits of earthly life. Before our spiritual sight appears the fact that we have shared in another life, in the spiritual world, prior to our present existence in the world of the senses; and in that spiritual life are to be found the real causes of the shaping of our physical existence. We become acquainted with the fact that before we received a physical body and entered upon this physical existence we lived a purely spiritual life. We see that that human being which we now are, with its faculties and inclinations, was prepared during a life that we spent in a purely spiritual world before birth. We look upon ourselves as upon beings who lived spiritually before their entrance into the world of the senses, and who are now striving to live as physical beings with those faculties and psychic characteristics which were originally attached to them and which have developed since their birth.

It would be a mistake to say: "How is it possible that in spiritual life I should have aspired to possess faculties and inclinations, which now, when I have got them, do not please me at all?" It does not matter whether something pleases the soul in the world of senses or not. That is not the point. The soul has quite different points of view for its aspirations in the spiritual world from those which it adopts in the life of the senses. The character of knowledge and will is quite different in the two worlds. In the spiritual life we know that for the sake of our total evolution we need a certain kind of life in the physical world, which when we get there may seem unsympathetic or depressing to the soul; and yet we strive for it, because in the spiritual existence we do not prefer what is sympathetic and agreeable, but what is necessary to the right development of our individual being.

It is the same with regard to the events of life. We contemplate them and see how we have prepared in the spiritual world what is antipathetic as well as what is sympathetic, and how we ourselves have brought together the impulses which cause our painful as well as our joyful experiences in physical existence. But even then we may find it incomprehensible that we ourselves have brought about this or that situation in life, as long as we only experience ourselves in the physical world. In the spiritual world, however, we have had what may be called supersensible insight which caused us to say: "You must go through that uncongenial or painful experience, for only such an experience can bring you a step further in your total development." From the standpoint of the physical world only, it is never possible to decide how far one particular life on earth brings a human being forward in his total evolution.

Having realised the spiritual existence that precedes our earthly existence, we see the reasons why in our spiritual life we have aimed at a certain kind of destiny for the ensuing terrestrial life. These reasons lead back to an earlier terrestrial life lived in the past. Upon the character of that earlier life, upon the experiences made and the capacities attained in it, depends the wish during the succeeding spiritual existence to correct defective experiences and develop neglected capacities through a new life upon earth. In the spiritual world you feel a wrong done by you to another human being to be a disturbance of the harmony of the world, and you realise the necessity of meeting that human being again on earth in the next terrestrial life, in order to be able to get into such relationship to him as to be able to repair the wrong you have done. During the progressive development of the soul the range of vision is widened over a whole series of earlier terrestrial lives. In this way you arrive through observation at a knowledge of the true history of the life of your higher "Ego." You see that man goes through his total existence in a succession of lives upon earth, and that between these repeated terrestrial lives he passes through purely spiritual states of existence which are connected with his terrestrial lives according to certain laws.

Thus the knowledge of repeated existences upon earth is lifted into the sphere of observation. (In order to avoid a frequently repeated mistake, attention is called to the following fact, more fully treated in other writings of mine. The sum total of a man's existence does not unfold itself in an endless repetition of lives. A certain number of repetitions take place, but both before the beginning and after the close of these quite different kinds of existence are found, and all this shows itself in its totality as a development inspired by sublime wisdom.)

The knowledge of repeated terrestrial lives may also be reached by reasonable observation of physical existence. In my books Theosophy and An Outline of Occult Science, as well as in lesser writings of mine, the attempt has been made to prove reincarnation along such lines of reasoning as are characteristic of the modern doctrine of evolution in natural science. It is there shown how logical thought and investigation that really follow up scientific research (and its results) to its full consequences are absolutely bound to accept the idea of evolution, presented to us by modern science, in such a sense as to consider the true being, the psychic individuality of man, as something which is evolving through a sequence of physical existences alternating with intermediate purely spiritual lives. The proofs attempted in those writings are naturally capable of much further development and completion. But the opinion does not seem unjustified that proofs in this matter have precisely the same scientific value as that which in general is called scientific proof. There is nothing in the science of spiritual things which cannot be confirmed by proofs of that kind. But of course we must admit the difficulty is greater for spiritually scientific proofs to be acknowledged than proofs of natural science.

This is not on account of their less stringent logic, but because in the face of such proofs one does not feel those underlying physical facts, which make the acceptance of the proofs of natural science so easy. This has nothing whatever to do with the conclusiveness of the reasoning itself. And if we are capable of comparing with an unbiased mind the proofs of natural science with those given on analogous lines by spiritual science, we shall easily be convinced of their equally conclusive power. Thus the force of such proofs may also be added to that which the investigator of the spiritual worlds has to give as a description of successive terrestrial lives resulting from his own vision. The one side can support the other in the formation of a conviction of the truth of human reincarnation based simply on reasonable comprehension. Here the attempt has been made to show the way that leads beyond mental comprehension to supersensible vision of this reincarnation.

Rudolf Steiner

* 9 7 8 9 3 5 7 9 9 0 3 0 1 *